2/

TV
Without
Cable

By
James Eldredge

Table of Contents

1 – Introduction

How much is your cable bill? I'm going to bet that it's somewhere around $50/month—or more, in a lot of cases. If you're getting anything beyond the basic TV package, it's probably closer to $100/month, all for a bunch of TV shows and movies that are punctuated with lots of advertisements that you're paying to watch. If you've ever wondered if there's a better (and cheaper) way to get entertained and informed, you're absolutely right. And in this book, you're going to learn all about it.

So what is 'it' exactly? It is called *streaming television* and it's taking the modern world by storm. Born from movie rental companies like Blockbuster, companies like Amazon, Netflix, Apple and Hulu have created a way for you to watch TV shows and movies on your computer, smartphone, tablet and—yes—your TV.

In many cases you don't even need any specialized equipment to start streaming. Many modern televisions come with applications built into them that let you connect to streaming services, and you can stream many services right onto your phone, tablet or computer.

The best part about streaming services is that most of them are either free or relatively inexpensive. In fact, I can virtually guarantee that getting yourself set up on multiple streaming services will be cheaper than your monthly cable bill. I'll use myself as an example of this.

I used to pay $100 every month for cable TV. That got me all the basic channels like news, a bit of sports and loads of TV shows and movies, plus my local channels. That wasn't all, though. I was also paying another $60 every month for high-speed internet access, making my monthly bill over $175 when you include taxes, fees, equipment rentals and all the other charges cable companies like to put in there.

These days, though? I'm paying around $53/month for all of the sports, news, weather, TV shows and movies I can handle. I could easily cut that down to around $20/month if I didn't like being able to play a non-stop stream of news and sports highlights in the background while I work.

So how did I do it? Simple! I cut the cable cord and embraced a life of 100% streaming. I'm no longer subject to cable TV's pricing, schedules or any other downsides. I can watch whatever I want whenever I want. I can pause, rewind and fast forward what I watch, too. My favorite part, though, has to be the fact that I don't have to see any ads anymore.

Does this sound interesting to you? Have you dreamed of something like this? If so, then prepare yourself. You're about to learn everything you need to know to cut the cable cord and start streaming!

2 – Streaming Differences

In the streaming world, there are three main types of streaming access available to you: free streaming, paid streaming, and OTA (over-the-air) streaming. In this section we'll discuss the pros/cons of each of these streaming types, along with some general information about streaming hardware that's useful to know.

Free Streaming

Free streaming is available for a wide variety of entertainment including TV shows both new and old, news and sports. Movies aren't generally available for free streaming except through sites that commit copyright infringement, and we want to stay far away from any illegal streaming methods.

In general, free streaming options are supported through advertisements, and you'll usually see a *lot* of them. For instance, some networks (ABC and CBS, for example) will make the latest episodes of their TV shows available to stream the day after they air, but you'll be forced to sit through commercials like you would if you were watching on TV. Nonetheless, this is still a great way to stay caught up on your favorite shows without having to subscribe to cable.

Paid Streaming

Paid streaming is where the real 'meat' of streaming happens. Popular TV shows and movies that are both old and new are available through services like Netflix, Sling TV, Amazon and iTunes, all without advertisements. Some services, like Hulu Plus, offer paid streaming services of newly released shows (the same day or day after they're aired on TV) but still carry the weight of advertisements.

The price of paid streaming options may seem daunting from time to time, but when you look at the value you get, regular cable TV service pales in comparison (and is more expensive, too!). You may have to subscribe to multiple paid streaming services to get access to all of the material you want to watch, but overall you should expect to save money.

Over-the-Air Streaming

Cable service generally includes access to local TV stations, which also broadcast a free signal that you can pick up with an antenna. Instead of relying on your cable TV service to deliver local news, sports and weather (along with other media), you can simply purchase an external antenna that's compatible with your TV and get all of these local channels for free.

Streaming Hardware

The last few years have brought an abundance of streaming devices to the market that help with watching streaming media on your TV. From televisions that have streaming apps built into them to devices like the Chromecast or Fire TV, there are plenty of ways to get streaming media onto your television. These types of devices are generally not necessary for internet-enabled devices like smartphones, tablets and computers, though, so if you plan to use streaming services exclusively on those types of devices, you shouldn't have to worry about purchasing any streaming hardware.

3 – Over-the-Air Streaming

To get started with over-the-air (OTA) streaming, it's helpful to know a bit about the history of the subject. Before cable and satellite started broadcasting local channels, the only way for you to get local channels was through an analog antenna. After the Federal Communications Commission changed the rules, though, all broadcast networks had to start broadcasting a digital signal. Cable companies take this signal and compress it and broadcast it as part of cable subscriptions, which is how you can get local channels through your cable TV subscription.

What Stations are in Your Area?

If you purchase a digital antenna and are within range of your local broadcast station, you'll be able to pick up the same signals—except better, because they aren't compressed. As long as you're close enough to the transmitter, you can get a *better* view of local stations through an antenna than you could through a cable subscription.

Most people who tap into OTA broadcasts will have access to several major stations such as ABC, CBS, Fox and others. Rural areas will be hit or miss for OTA signals, though, and you won't know what stations are available near you unless you do a bit of research first.

One of the best ways to find out what stations are available in your area for OTA streaming is by visiting a website like **TV Fool** (tvfool.com). If you enter your address, you'll be able to see what OTA channels are in your area, along with an estimation of what kind of signal strength you can expect to see.

Another great resource for both finding out what channels you can expect to receive at your location as well as great recommendations for which antenna to buy is **AntennaWeb** (antennaweb.org). By submitting your street address and zip code, you'll get a map and color-coded result that shows you both what channels are in the area and where they're broadcasting from.

To get right to the 'official' source of transmission maps, you can also visit the **FCC's map page** (transition.fcc.gov/mb/engineering/dtvmaps/), where you can enter in your address and see a list of digital stations that are broadcasting in your area. This gives similar information to what you'll find on AntennaWeb, but without the directional information that AntennaWeb provides.

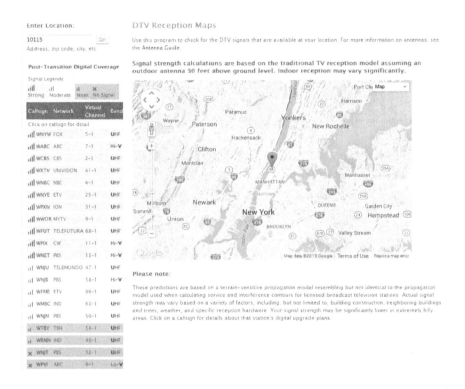

Choosing the Right Antenna

Now that you know which local stations you can expect to pick up through OTA streaming, it's time to get your hands on a digital TV antenna. These vary in price depending on size, but you can generally find them for anywhere between $20 to $50 depending on what you choose. I personally opted for a 35-mile **Amazon Basics model** (amzn.com/B00DIFIP06), which has worked fantastically where I live on the Gulf Coast. Your mileage may vary, though, so try out AntennaWeb's antenna recommendation engine to help you choose what's best for you.

Generally speaking, if you live in an urban environment, an un-powered antenna like the Amazon Basics model should work perfectly fine for picking up OTA streams. If you live in a more rural area, though, you may need to purchase an amplified antenna. These antennas use an external power source to amplify the signal they receive, which can both help and hinder in the reception of OTA signals. Because everything is amplified, if the antenna picks up any interference, that interference will be amplified as well, potentially resulting in a poor picture quality.

On the upside, if you live far away from the source of the transmission you want to watch, an amplifier can be the difference between not being able to pick up the transmission and being able to do so. That's why it's important to do your research through a resource like AntennaWeb before purchasing your antenna, so that you can get the best possible quality for your OTA streaming.

4 – Paid Streaming Services

Legal Streaming

Are you ready to get started on this awesome journey towards streaming TV? Awesome! Before we get started, let's clarify what we mean by 'free & paid streaming services.' We aren't going to be talking about anything illegal here. We aren't going to discuss Bittorrent, illegal streaming services or other illicit methods of watching TV shows and movies. What we *are* going to talk about is a collection of paid and free sites and services that will give you a wide variety of entertainment and information.

Pros & Cons of Streaming Services

As was alluded to earlier in this book, there are both some upsides and downsides to getting rid of your cable service and switching only to streaming services. Some of the pros include a lower cost, watching what you want when you want and having access to a wide variety of media. Some of the cons include the fact that you'll need a constant high-speed internet connection to watch streaming services, you'll be using up a lot of data on your connection (no cellphone data plans allowed here!) and you'll be a *bit* behind live TV with most (but not all) streaming services.

With a few exceptions, most streaming services lag anywhere from a few days to a few months (or more) behind cable TV in terms of broadcast times. For example, with cable TV you can watch episodes of your favorite show as they air every week. With Netflix, though, you might have to wait until the season is finished before you can watch it. With Hulu, you might have to wait an extra day or two. With Sling TV, you can watch TV live just like it was a cable TV broadcast. Whether or not you can put up with these types of potential delays is entirely up to you. Speaking from personal experience, though, I don't mind having to wait a while to watch new shows if it means my cable bill is cut in half. And for some shows I don't even have to wait!

Before you go and cut your cable service, you should also check and make sure that your high-speed internet is really 'high-speed' and that you don't have a data cap in place. A DSL-speed connection is what I'd consider the absolute bare minimum for viewing streaming media, but even then you're going to have to deal with latency, long load times and other speed-related issues. A cable connection should be just fine for streaming media, and as long as you've got an unlimited data allotment, you're good to go. If you're not sure if you have unlimited data on your internet plan, call up your provider and ask them about it. As competition slowly increases for entrenched providers, more and more areas are starting to have their data caps removed, which is only good news for you.

Amazon Prime ($8.25/month)

Amazon Prime (amazon.com/dp/B00DBYBNEE) has more value than most other services put together, all thanks to the fact that for $99/year you get access to free 2-day shipping on items you buy on Amazon, free book rentals, free music streaming and, yes, free TV show and movie streaming as well.

About Amazon Prime

Receive all the benefits of Amazon Prime including FREE Two-Day Shipping for eligible purchases, unlimited streaming of movies and TV shows with Prime Instant Video, and the ability to borrow books from the Kindle Owners' Lending Library for $99 a year.

The benefits include:

- **FREE Two-Day Shipping** on eligible items to addresses in the contiguous U.S. and other shipping benefits. For more information, go to Amazon Prime Shipping Benefits.
- **FREE Same-Day Delivery** in eligible zip codes. For more information, go to Order with Prime FREE Same-Day Delivery.
- **Prime Instant Video**: unlimited streaming of movies and TV episodes for paid or free trial members in the U.S. and Puerto Rico. For more information, go to About Prime Instant Video.
- **Prime Music**: unlimited, ad-free access to hundreds of Prime Playlists and more than a million songs for members in the U.S. and Puerto Rico. For more information, go to About Prime Music.
- **Prime Photos**: Secure unlimited photo storage in Amazon Cloud Drive. For more information, go to About Prime Photos.
- **Prime Pantry**: Access to Prime Pantry, where members can purchase and ship to addresses in the contiguous U.S. low priced grocery, household, and pet care items for a flat delivery fee of $5.99 for each Prime Pantry box. Prime Pantry orders cannot be shipped to addresses in Alaska, Hawaii, and Puerto Rico.
- **Amazon Elements**: Access to Amazon Elements products, Amazon's own line of everyday essentials.
- **Prime Early Access**: Get 30-minute early access to Lightning Deals on Amazon.com and new events on MyHabit.com. For more information, go to About Prime Early Access.
- **Kindle Owners' Lending Library**: access to members in the U.S. For more information, go to Kindle Owners' Lending Library
- **Kindle First**: Early access for members in the U.S. to download a new book for free every month from the Kindle First picks. For more information, go to Kindle First.
- **Membership Sharing**: Two adults living in the same household can create an Amazon Household to share certain Amazon Prime benefits. For more information, go to About Amazon Households.

Leaving aside all of those other upsides, though, let's talk about the pros and cons of Amazon's Prime Video service.

With several thousand movies and TV shows to watch, including some shows that were created by Amazon and have won several awards,

Amazon has a huge collection of media that's right at your fingertips. Amazon's video service integrates perfectly with their range of Fire TV devices and Kindle Fire tablets, and they rotate content in and out fairly frequently, ensuring that you'll always have something new to watch. Their original content is no joke, either, and this has been made crystal clear with their signing of the hosts of the UK version of Top Gear to a multi-million dollar contract to produce no less than *three* new shows that will air on Amazon.

So what's the downside? Honestly, I don't see a big downside to Amazon Prime. The only negative that I can come up with is that the streaming music and video interface when you're on a computer is pretty terrible. Netflix is the gold standard for web browser streaming interfaces, and Amazon's interface falls far short. Still, though, when you're watching on anything *but* a computer web browser, the experience is awesome, and I can wholeheartedly recommend this as a must-have for your streaming media collection.

Oh, one last side note. If you ever want to purchase movies, shows or even entire seasons of shows, you can do that through Amazon as well. You'll gain access to a download of your purchase, and you'll be able to stream it from your media library anytime as well. These purchases are obviously separate from Amazon's Prime streaming offerings, but it's good to know about them, too.

Netflix ($8-$12/month)

Ah yes, **Netflix** (netflix.com). The gold standard in streaming services, and the 'original' streaming service that some say was responsible for driving Blockbuster out of business. With three plans to choose from at either $8, $9 or $12 per month, Netflix offers a fantastic bargain and is compatible with virtually any internet-enabled device that's ever been made. They rotate out shows and movies on a monthly basis and have several original series, many of which have won awards and are amazingly well produced. These original programs like Orange is the New Black and House of Cards don't get rotated out of Netflix, and are released seasonally, meaning you can binge on an entire season at once or spread them out and watch them one at a time, whichever you want to do!

When you look at the Netflix streaming plans, it's important to note the differences between the levels, which are mainly the number of screens you can watch at the same time and the availability of HD and Ultra HD.

NETFLIX

Choose the plan that's right for you

Downgrade or upgrade at any time

	Basic	Standard	Premium
Price after free month ends	$7.99	$8.99	$11.99
HD available	✗	✓	✓
Ultra HD (when available)	✗	✗	✓
Screens you can watch on at the same time	1	2	4
Watch on your laptop, TV, phone and tablet	✓	✓	✓
Unlimited movies and TV shows	✓	✓	✓
Cancel anytime	✓	✓	✓
First month free	✓	✓	✓

High Definition (HD) and Ultra High Definition (Ultra HD) availability subject to your Internet service and device capabilities. Not all content available in HD or Ultra HD. See Terms of Use for more details.

Continue

Prices updated Aug 2015

For $8/month you can watch Netflix on one screen at a time, and you'll only get SD (standard definition) transmission of shows and movies. While you might be tempted by this option due to the low price, I'd caution you not to fall prey to it so easily. If there's more than one person in your household who will be using Netflix, it's going to be impossible for them to watch a show at the same time you are watching one if you go with this plan. Additionally, a SD transmission is going to

21

look *awful* on a modern TV. On a modern HD television, SD content looks fuzzy and pixelated, which is just plain unenjoyable to watch.

For just $1/month more, though, you can go with the Standard plan, which is what I personally use. It lets you watch Netflix on two screens at once, which lets me watch a movie in the living room on the TV at the same time as my wife watches a TV show in the bedroom on her laptop. You also get full HD with the Standard plan, so shows will look crisp and clear on your TV, tablet, laptop, smartphone or wherever else you're watching. In my opinion, the Standard plan is the best deal, and is well worth the money.

For $12/month you can subscribe to the Premium plan, which gives you an Ultra HD transmission (when available) and lets up to 4 different screens be streaming from Netflix at the same time. This plan is really only for those with a family that loves streaming all the time, or those with an Ultra HD 4K television. If you don't fit into either of those two categories save yourself $3/month and stick with the Standard plan for $9/month. You won't be gaining anything with the Premium plan.

Hulu Plus ($8-$17/month)

While **Hulu** (hulu.com/start) offers a free viewing option, most of its content is locked behind a paywall that costs $8 per month to access. For an extra $9 per month you can get access to 'SHOWTIME' content, all without commercial content.

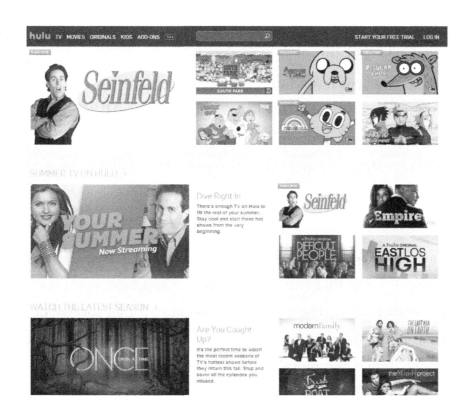

That 'without commercial content' bit is actually really important, because it only applies to the 'SHOWTIME' subscription. When you subscribe to Hulu Plus, you'll still have to watch commercials, and lots of them. Whether you're watching reruns of Seinfeld or Survivor or you're catching up on last night's episode of The Bachelorette or CSI, all of the shows on Hulu Plus come with advertisements, even if you're already paying them a monthly fee.

If this seems eerily similar to how cable companies work, you're not wrong. Both companies charge you a fee to view content, and pile ads on top of it. The key difference here is that with Hulu Plus, you'll be paying much less per month than you would for your cable TV subscription, plus you'll have on-demand access to a HUGE amount of shows. So instead of having to schedule your viewing of your favorite show around when it airs on cable, you can just watch it whenever you want on Hulu Plus.

The other major benefit to getting Hulu Plus instead of sticking with Hulu's free shows is that Hulu free is only viewable in a computer web browser. Hulu Plus, on the other hand, has apps for all sorts of devices, so you can watch Hulu Plus shows on your smart TV, streaming device, smartphone, tablet and more. If you like to sprawl out on the couch in front of the TV while watching your shows (I know I do!) then Hulu Plus is what you'll want to get. Keep in mind, though, that not *all* shows may be watchable on every device. Licensing agreements are complicated, and the rights holders for each show can decide where the shows can be played. It's frustrating, I know, but you can still get a fair amount of use out of Hulu, even if you don't get Hulu Plus.

By the way, if you're confused about which shows are free to watch on Hulu and which require a Hulu Plus subscription, just look in the upper left corner of the show's thumbnail. Shows that you can watch for free without a subscription won't have anything there, but shows that require Hulu Plus will have a green rectangle that looks like this:

SUBSCRIBE

iTunes (Price Varies)

As strange as it may seem (given the fact that **iTunes** (apple.com/itunes) is usually thought of as a music service), iTunes is a very viable option for purchasing TV shows and movies. At least in theory.

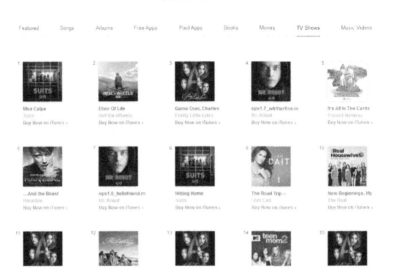

The biggest problem with iTunes is actually a collection of problems. First, there's no all-in-one monthly price option like you see with Netflix, Hulu Plus or Amazon Prime. You have to rent or purchase each show or movie individually.

Once you do, the next problem begins. Unless you own an Apple TV or you're okay with watching your media through the iTunes app on your computer, you'll have to jump through a lot of hoops to watch your purchased content on any other device.

You can either mirror your display to your TV or another device from your computer, or you can try to go through the arduous process of breaking the file encryption on the files that you legally purchased just so you can watch them wherever you want.

Unless you're 100% committed to Apple's ecosystem and have zero interest in diversifying, iTunes really isn't a very good choice at all for streaming media. iTunes itself is clunky, slow and bloated and the limitations that are put on your own media are enough to drive even the most patient person mind-bogglingly crazy.

Sling TV ($20-$45/month)

Sling TV (sling.com) is the new kid on the block as far as streaming services go, and it's one of the most TV-like streaming experiences you'll see.

SLING TV PACKAGES

Package	Price	Channels
The Best of Live TV (core)	$20 per month	ESPN, ESPN2, AMC, TNT, TBS, CNN, A&E, Lifetime, History, Food Network, HGTV, Travel Channel, Cartoon Network/Adult Swim, Disney Channel, ABC Family, IFC, H2, El Rey Network, Maker, Galavision
Sports Extra	$5	SEC Network, ESPNEWS, ESPNU, Universal Sports, Univision Deportes, beIN Sports, ESPN Buzzer Beater, ESPN Bases Loaded, ESPN Goal Line
Kids Extra	$5	Disney Junior, Disney XD, Boomerang, Baby TV, Duck TV
Lifestyle Extra	$5	truTV, Cooking Channel, DIY, WE tv, FYI, LMN
World News Extra	$5	Bloomberg TV, HLN, Euro News, France 24, NDTV 24/7, News 18, Russia Today
Hollywood Extra	$5	EPIX, EPIX2, EPIX3, EPIX Drive-In, Sundance TV

Pricing information taken from Cnet.com, Aug 2015

With a base price of $20 per month, you get access to Sling's 'core' channels, which is quite a full-featured list on its own. With $5 per month addons, though, you can get more news, sports, kids and other genre channels, as seen above. HBO is also available through Sling, too and with an extra $15 per month you'll be able to watch HBO's live shows, which is great for fans of Game of Thrones!

The biggest downside to Sling TV is that it behaves (essentially) exactly like regular live TV, except for the fact that it's much cheaper. Aside from a select group of programs, you can't record or rewind live shows, and you're stuck watching what's on according to the normal TV airtime schedule, along with a minute or two delay. This might not be a problem for you if you're comfortable with a cable TV or OTA TV viewing schedule, though, so it's really up to your personal preference.

Aside from that, though, Sling TV is fantastic! You are limited to only one stream, so you can't watch it on two devices at the same time, but that's similar to cable TV as well. For news and sports, you can't beat Sling's pricing, considering that you can get the awesome basic package, the news package and the sports package all for just $35 per month. With that, you'll be able to watch the latest episodes of your favorite shows from channels like TBS, ABC Family, movies on TNT, cartoons on Cartoon Network as well as get news from CNN, Bloomberg and RU along with sports from ESPN, US, Univision and more.

If you're still determined to stay with live television, Sling TV is the best substitute for cable TV that you'll find on the market today. The excellent package and pricing options are top-notch and offer real value at a price that will still save you money on your cable subscription, even if you were to subscribe to all of them at once!

HBO Now ($15/month)

Now this is quite interesting. Exclusive to Apple at first, **HBO Now** (order.hbonow.com) is available on a much wider variety of devices.

For $15 per month you can gain full access to HBO's library of shows, and in an on-demand format, no less. Unlike OTA, Sling or traditional cable subscriptions, once a show airs on HBO Now you can watch it whenever you want (like Amazon Prime or Netflix).

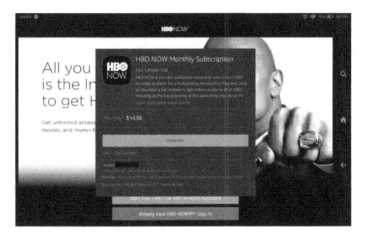

Kindle Fire HBO NOW signup page, Aug 2015

In order to sign up for HBO Now, you have to do so through a 'provider' such as Amazon, Apple or Google. This is a slightly confusing method, but it's like that due to a complex set of licensing agreements HBO has for its content. In the above screenshot you can see that by downloading the free HBO Now app from Amazon's Appstore, you can sign up for a $15 per month subscription to HBO Now through Amazon's Appstore.

HBO Now does come with a free month trial through every provider I checked (that's subject to change, though, depending on the whims of HBO and the providers themselves, of course), and no matter where you sign up, your cost should only be $15 per month. If you don't have any interest in HBO's offerings, there's absolutely no reason for you to get HBO Now. For those who have clung to their cable TV subscription solely because of HBO, though, this is a way to quickly get out of your cable TV subscription and still get access to the shows you love.

5 – Free Streaming Services & Streaming News Services

Now that we've looked at the variety of paid streaming services that are available, let's look at a few free ones as well. Keep in mind that legal free streaming services are few and far between, mostly due to the fact that it's hard for a streaming site to survive financially on advertising alone. As a result, any free streaming sites will be delivering a *lot* of ads, so be prepared for that.

Hulu

If you've read through chapter 4, you'll remember that Hulu Plus was mentioned as a decent streaming service with some serious downsides. If you haven't read that chapter yet, I encourage you to do so, as some of what we'll be talking about here depends on information contained in that chapter.

Ready to go? Awesome! So with **Hulu** (hulu.com), if you see a show there that does *not* have a green 'Subscribe' button on it, that means that you can watch the show without having to purchase a Hulu Plus subscription. There are a fair amount of shows available on Hulu for free, but the catch for some of them is that they switch to requiring a

Hulu Plus subscription a few days or weeks after airing. This means that you can catch some of your favorite shows for free (with lots of commercials, of course), but only for so long.

Network-Specific Streams, Including News

If you're located in certain geographic areas, some networks (like ABC or CBS) offer both paid and free streaming options. With ABC, for example, if you live in an area where they've enabled free streaming, you can view the latest episodes of ABC's shows on their **website** (abc.go.com). The best way to find streams like this is to search on your favorite search engine for a phrase like '*networkname streaming shows*'.

This is also a great way to get ahold of news streams that some networks offer. While most major networks don't offer a 24/7 free stream, they do offer free highlights and news summaries that are updated regularly, and which are free to stream from their websites. If you visit the video pages of CNN, Fox, CBS, ABC or other news networks (including ones outside the USA) you'll usually find highlights that you can stream, and sometimes even a full livestream. This also applies to local affiliate stations in your area, though they generally won't live stream their broadcast except in severe weather situations or during emergencies.

"Other" Streams

When searching for streams for news, shows or movies online, you might be tempted to try some of "those" sites that appear in the search results. By "those" sites, of course, I mean "questionably legal" ones that may be either on the border of legality or that are blatantly breaking copyright law.

While some of these sites can provide shows, movies, news, sports and other free streams, the downsides are enormous. Websites such as these are frequent targets for hackers, who can either bring the site down or install malicious software that will automatically download to your computer when you visit.

The advertising on these sites is usually horrendous as well, with popup ads, ads that cover most of the screen and ads throughout the videos. Add to this the fact that most of these types of sites provide video that's extremely low quality and pretty soon you're left with the fact that they're just not worth visiting. I know it's tempting, but believe me when I tell you that the risks and downsides far outweigh any benefits you might get.

6 – Sports Streaming

So far, aside from Sling TV, we haven't talked about how you can watch sports. Cable TV packages can include a *lot* of different sports channels, and that's an important part of many people's lives. If you're someone who can't live without seeing every game, read on for some places where you can purchase live sports streams for the MLB, NFL and NBA.

NFL Game Pass ($100/month)

The NFL has been slow to evolve to streaming TV over the years, but **Game Pass** (nfl.com/gamepass) is the best thing to come along in a long time. For a cost of $100 per month, you get access to live preseason games and replays of all 256 regular season games whenever you want, on-demand and in high definition. While you can't watch regular NFL games live with Game Pass, this is the only (legal) way to get access to the games without going through a cable or satellite TV subscription.

FEATURES

MULTIPLE DEVICES

Watch on desktop or in NFL Mobile, coming soon to connected TVs

LIVE GAMEDAY AUDIO

Listen live to every NFL game - including the Playoffs and Super Bowl 50

NO SPOILERS

Use the Scores On/Off feature to hide the scores for all games

CONDENSED GAMES

Look back on entire NFL games in about 30 minutes

THOUSANDS OF GAMES

Full replays of games from 2009-present, commercial free in HD

COACHES FILM

Analyze the game like a pro with exclusive All-22 and EndZone angles

NFL PLAYOFFS

Watch the 2015 NFL Playoffs and Super Bowl 50 On-Demand

PREMIUM VIDEO

Access replays of NFL television programs and films

Game Pass does come with a 7-day free trial, and can play on your smartphone, tablet or computer. It's not yet available for smart televisions, though the **NFL Game Pass website** (nfl.com/gamepass) does say (as of Aug 2015) that it's 'coming soon.' There are also local and national blackout restrictions that you'll have to contend with, along with the fact that the fine print says that 'NFL Game Pass includes live access to *most* preseason games' (emphasis mine). You can read more about the details of NFL Game Pass on their **help page** (nfl.com/game-pass-help) to see if it's right for you.

MLB.tv ($20-$25/month)

MLB.tv's prices change… a lot. Some source peg the monthly price at much higher than $25 month, while the current (as of Aug 2015) pricing is either $20 per month or $25 per month, depending on what plan you want. These prices change pretty frequently from the looks of things, so be sure to check out the **MLB subscription page** (mlb.mlb.com/mlb/subscriptions/) for the latest prices before you sign up.

2015 Regular Season Features	MLB.tv PREMIUM	MLB.tv
Includes **At Bat** Premium for Free (Watch on Mobile Devices) Learn more »	✔	
Watch on Connected Devices (Roku, XBox, Apple TV, Sony...) Learn more »	✔	
Choice of Home or Away Feeds Learn more »	✔	
New for 2015 ‹ Watch on Playstation Vita and Playstation TV Learn more »	✔	
Now Available ‹ Web-based HD Media Player Learn more »	✔	✔
New for 2015 ‹ Audio Overlay / Spanish Audio Sync Learn more »	✔	✔
HD Picture Learn more »	✔	✔
LIVE Game DVR Learn more »	✔	✔
Multi-Game Viewing Learn more »	✔	✔
More + Learn more »	✔	✔
Buy Now	$49.99/year $24.99/month	$39.99/year $19.99/month

In terms of subscriptions, there are two to choose from: MLB.tv and
MLB.tv Premium. The first costs $20 per month and lets you watch the
game on your computer and you get access to 'every out-of-market
game LIVE online.' MLB.tv premium, however, lets you watch games
on a multitude of devices (over 400 supported according to the MLB.tv

FAQ) and lets you watch both home and away games, whichever you want.

MLB.tv subscriptions are, of course, subject to blackout subscriptions, so if you only like watching one team and you live near them, you probably don't want to subscribe to MLB.tv, and instead pick up the games through OTA broadcast.

To determine which games you *can't* see due to blackout restrictions, visit **mlb.mlb.com/mlb/subscriptions/#blackout** and enter your zip code in the specified box, then click the green 'Go' button. You'll then be presented with a list of teams that will be blacked out for you, regardless of whether they are playing at home or away. Since MLB.tv doesn't offer a free trial, I'd strongly recommend that you make use of this blackout checker before signing up so that you don't end up disappointed.

NBA League Pass ($7-$200)

Unlike the NFL and MLB's monthly subscription offerings, the NBA only offers a single-purchase option, with three different tiers. The first lets you purchase streaming access to a single game for $7. The middle tier lets you purchase access to all of a specified team's games for $120. The highest tier gives you 'full' access to the league's games for $200 for the season. These prices are for the 2015-16 season, and might change for future seasons, of course.

Games through NBA League Pass are broadcast live, so there's no waiting for an archive to become available. You can also view them on your smartphone, tablet, computer, streaming device or smart TV. Blackout rules once again strike, though, and at the bottom of the **NBA League Pass page** (nba.com/leaguepass/) you can find a handy zip code blackout list lookup tool. It's also worth pointing out that any games that are nationally broadcast on NBATV, ABC, ESPN or TNT are blacked out for NBA League Pass. If you only follow one team and they're nearby, you'll probably want to skip NBA League Pass and just catch the games on a local broadcast.

7 – Streaming Devices

Now that you have a variety of resources for getting media online instead of through a cable subscription, we should talk about streaming devices and how they can be of value to you. "But wait," you say, "all of the streaming services we talked about will work on my computer! And most work on my smartphone and tablet, and some even work on my smart television!"

While that's very true, the fact remains that a lot of people (myself included) prefer to watch shows and movies on my TV, instead of on my phone or computer. Also, not everyone has a smart TV, and even if you do, it might not support all of the streaming services that you subscribe to. The fact is that due to the low price of streaming devices, it's very cost-effective to purchase one, connect it to your TV and use that as your media hub, since most streaming devices will support most streaming services. Which streaming device you choose it up to you, but I'll cover my top two streaming devices and explain what makes them so great. (There are lots of others, of course, but covering every single streaming device would take a full book just by itself!)

Amazon Fire TV ($100)

've tried just about every streaming device on the market, but the one
hat I use for day-to-day life is my **Amazon Fire TV**
amazon.com/dp/B00CX5P8FC). It natively plays all of my Amazon
Prime music, movies and TV shows, as well as all of the media I've
purchased from Amazon over the years.

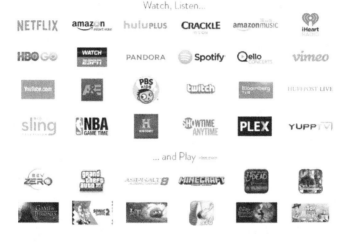

There's a big app library, including apps for things like HBO, Netflix,
NBA League Pass, Hulu Plus, Sling TV and more. The Fire TV is also
ock solid, rarely needing a restart, and when I'm looking for a
particular piece of media or an app, I can use the remote control's
microphone to do a voice search instead of having to slowly type out

what I'm searching for using a 4-way directional control. The Fire TV has an HDMI out port, along with an optical audio out port as well, supporting 5.1 surround sound.

If you don't want to drop $100 on a Fire TV, you can always consider the **Fire TV Stick** (amazon.com/dp/B00GDQ0RMG) instead. It only costs $40, and has many of the same features as the Fire TV. The major differences are that the remote has no microphone (so no audio searches), there's no optical output port on the stick, and it runs significantly slower than the Fire TV. The times when I've used the Fire TV Stick, I've noticed the speed difference between it and my Fire TV, and it's enough to drive me back to the Fire TV every time. Nonetheless, it still supports a wide range of streaming apps and is a great choice as long as you don't mind it being a bit sluggish at times.

If you're looking for a guide book for the Fire TV or Fire TV Stick, I recommend **these** (amzn.com/B00JHVHQU0) two **books** (amzn.com/B00JHVHQU0) from Amazon. They're written by a good friend of mine, Charles Tulley, and are top-rated and updated monthly

Chromecast ($35)

Google's **Chromecast** (amzn.com/ B00DR0PDNE) is comparable to Amazon's Fire TV Stick, but with a few key differences. First off is that there's no remote included; you'll be controlling the Chromecast from your smartphone or tablet instead. While the Chromecast also supports streaming media apps like MLB.tv, HBO Go, Hulu Plus and Netflix, it doesn't natively support streaming Amazon Prime video. Instead, you have to '**cast**' (google.com/chrome/devices/chromecast/learn.html) Amazon videos, along with other media, to the Chromecast.

What's this 'casting' all about? Well, Chromecast was designed as a streaming media *receiver* that would take media streamed to it from your computer or smartphone and then display that media on your TV. This process isn't super complicated, but it's enough of a hassle that I prefer to either use native apps or, if what I want to watch isn't supported by a native app, switch back over to a different device.

One of the best resources I've found for digging into the Chromecast and learning how to 'cast' properly is over at **ChromecastHelp.com**. I'm not affiliated with them, but their help guides have been a tremendous resource for the times when I've used or helped other people use a Chromecast.

Other Devices

There are many other streaming devices available that all do roughly the same thing, but with emphasis on different features. The **Apple TV** (apple.com/appletv), for example, is very closed and focuses mainly on streaming content purchased through iTunes. The **Roku** (roku.com) is one of the first 'original' streaming devices and focuses on delivering new apps as often as possible, which often take a while to filter out to other devices. Finally, if you have a PS3, PS4 or Xbox One game console, those can act as fantastic streaming devices, too! All three of these consoles have apps that deliver content from Netflix, HBO, Hulu, various sports services and more!

Choosing the Best Device for You

Ultimately, your choice of a streaming media device comes down to one thing: you. If you're an Apple fanatic and are locked into iTunes, then an Apple TV is probably the best device for you. If you have an Amazon Prime subscription and enjoy watching streaming media from Amazon, then a Fire TV would be great. If you enjoy trying out new apps and getting access to cutting-edge features, why not try a Roku? Different devices are designed with emphasis in different areas, so whichever one best matches your needs is the one you should go with.

8 – Wrapping it All Up

We've covered a lot in this book, and I'm hopeful that it was both educational and useful! We've covered various streaming devices, looked at the pros and cons of many different streaming services and talked at length about how to effectively pick up an OTA (over-the-air) broadcast signal.

Armed with this new knowledge, you should feel confident and well-equipped to cut your ties with cable TV and venture forth into the land of streaming. It may feel strange at first, but the benefits you'll receive are vast. As technology continues to develop and companies continue to move towards streaming media, you'll only see better and better options for streaming, and costs will (hopefully) continue to drop.

If you enjoyed this book and found it helpful, please do consider leaving a review for it at Amazon. Reviews are one of the best ways readers find new books, and sharing your experience with other potential readers would be of great value to me.

If you'd like to stay up to date with some great free tech books, I encourage you to sign up for the AppSna.gr newsletter at **appsna.gr/hdxtips**.

I've partnered with them to offer my books for free through their book giveaway program, so each time I write a new book, review copies are randomly given out to dozens of folks who are subscribed to the newsletter.

Made in United States
Orlando, FL
09 February 2024

43510973R00036